# Preface

My idea began when I came home from work in the late afternoon and my wife was watching a talk show (Oprah!) on how widespread online predators were all across America. I was disturbed at how many young people get in trouble online.

I have a interesting job as an Information Security Specialist and this alerts me of some of the dangers. As a father myself, I understand that parents today are busy. I wanted to make a useful and straight forward guide on what parents can do to help keep their computers and families safe. So, I did some research of what information is out there for busy parents and what they can do to help keep their children safe when using the internet and other technologies.

This book is designed for you – the average, not too-technical parent. You want to reasonably understand the technology that your families use.

Your want to know more about your home computer, what's going on thru your internet connection, what can be done with your or your kids cellular phone (which at least has text messaging and probably many internet capable features)

You understand that the computer-connected world is a very interesting place with beneficial information. But some serious threats exist ... the news tells of online predators, luring kids, identity theft, privacy concerns, even cyber-bullying.

Whether you have a Windows PC, Mac, a cellular phone that has Internet capabilities , or the shiny I-Phone, the threats are out there..

As a parent, you want to know about the risks and what you can do to protect your family. The intent of this booklet is not just about spying on our kids - it's better to build an environment of communication and trust with them. It's designed in a concise manner to educate the average busy parent.

We hope that in one nights reading, a parent can be much more equipped to keep their family safer in today's cyber-world. As well, there are many helpful tips, links, suggestions websites, and resources for today's parent.

# Title

By Kris Jmaeff

Copyright 2009 by author.

ISBN **1441490434**

First Printing - February 17, 2009

# Table of Contents

# Introduction

In the name of protecting our families and security – we lock our doors and cars, have deadbolts, alarms, car immobilizers, cameras, dogs…

We watch the food that we feed our families   and look for unsafe additives or chemicals…

We teach our kids to not to talk to strangers or accept candy or gifts from someone we don't know….

In the same way, you don't want to leave your computer that our families use  - wide open to anyone.

A  general problem of internet security is that a  person can very easily impersonate someone he or she is not. It is very hard for you to  really know and trust that the person you are chatting with online is actually the person they claim to be.

The household computer contains personal information. Not just your shopping habits, your friend's emails and what sites you look at for fun but also could have banking, tax, and other confidential information. Your kids could unknowingly release private information to unsavory online rogues or (worse yet) predators..

Kids are using  to the Internet more and more everyday, playing games, communicating with  friends (whether it is texting, emailing, blogging, chatting), recording their thoughts and experiences (blogging, social networking), and researching their  homework.

 The Internet has opened up a whole new world for them.

 However, this online world, like the real world, is made up of a wide array of people.

Most are nice and decent , but some may be rude, obnoxious, insulting, or even mean and exploitative.

There also is an influences  of sex, violence, drugs, criminal activities, and other adult themes that could be dangerous for them.

There are even legal implications of owning or using a computer.

Many people don't realize the extent of the problems they could face when their computers aren't protected and their family is not informed.

For example, parents don't realize that if their children or children's friends use their computer for illegal activities (illegal downloads, harassment, fraud), they could be the ones legally responsible for the crime since the machine is registered under their name and in their house.

The fact that there are dangers online, however, is not a reason to avoid using these services.

It would be extreme to rid your household of all computers, phones and the internet.

As a parent - you can set family rules and guidelines for other aspects of interaction with society. You should also do the same with online activity and minimize the risks that are out there.

Children need supervision and practical advice on how to make their activity on the Internet a happy, healthy, and productive one.

This book is designed to be an informative, easy to understand and a clear source of advice that an average parent can use. We want you to protect your family in the information world.

There are many ways that a user can communicate on the internet.

---

Each Chapter:

     - explains the activity and what you can do
     -outlines the different technologies that are commonly used
     -details the main risks
     -has suggestions on how you can protect your family

# Web sites

WWW is short for the World Wide Web - is the most popular place to visit on the Internet

A Web site consists of a "page," or a collection of pages, containing text, pictures, links for downloading games, music or software and sound and video clips. There are literally millions of sites on the Web, which can be accessed using software on your computer called a Web "browser."

Common browsers are Microsoft's Internet Explorer, Mozilla Firefox and Google Chrome.

The Web also has sites that are 'user defined content' (Wikipedia, Facebook, etc)– it offers anyone the ability to create their own custom content.

Young people use the Web to explore and display their creativity in very exciting ways - creating online movies, music, Web sites, and blogs or online diaries. (See blogging and social networking )

Wikipedia is a growing internet phenomena  - it is a wealth of information  - it calls itself a free online encyclopedia  that anyone can edit.  It has rules and guidelines that users can follow and update any topic with any new bits of information.

However, the Web has its downside.

When surfing it's easy to come across sites containing pornography, messages that inspire hatred or prejudice, violence or  illegal content and activities.

 Children's privacy can be at risk both from commercial sites that ask for personal information, and when kids themselves post contact information or personal photos.

(this practice is very common especially with cell phones and social networking sites)

It can take only a few seconds with the proper software  to post a photo from their cell phone on the internet for all to see.

With millions of pages already published, and thousands more being posted every day, finding accurate online information can be an intimidating task. Since anyone can publish their views online, the Web contains a great deal of inaccurate and misleading information.

There is the danger that young people tend to believe that "if it's on a computer it must be true," so it's important to teach your kids to question what they read online.

If your kids have their own Web sites, be aware of what they are posting. Teach them to respect copyright by not stealing from other sites and to never post anything threatening about another person.

## You can check visited web sites

Viewing the log of visited web sites can give you enough information about your kid's habits, interests and online friends. Normally you should do this only occasionally but if your child becomes secretive, then you might want to check more often. If you find that the history of sites visited is deleted in your Web Browser, this is a signal that something might be going on. You should investigate. There are several ways you can do that later on in this chapter.

## At what age should I let my children go on the Internet?

Children are going online at younger and younger ages – even pre-schoolers!

Many kids are using the Internet at school by six years of age, so realistically, they will probably want to be going online at home around this age as well. Children under ten, however, generally don't have the critical thinking skills to be online alone, so until this age you must be totally involved in their Internet use. Sit with them whenever they are online. Make sure they only go to sites you have chosen. Teach them to never reveal personal information over the Internet.

Of course, older kids may need more frequent access perhaps for school projects. This will make them more responsible in using the Internet.

Be aware – It's very easy for a child to gain access to the internet other than home: school, library, a computer store, a friends house, even a friends cell phone!

Sit down with your child and agree on types of websites your child may and may not visit and limit the use of Instant Messaging and chat rooms.

Set guidelines and limit your children to visiting only certain websites, social networking sites or chat rooms. More on how to do this later on..

**What house rules should I have for Internet use?**

Many parents believe that rules have a positive effect on young peoples behavior. When your kids are very young – it's suggested that you always sit with them when they are online.

When they get a little older it is helpful to create a safe, personalized online environment by limiting your kids to their list of favorite or "bookmarked" sites. This can be done by allowing them only to use kid-friendly sites or search engines. There are even services that offer kid-friendly email programs (www.zoobuh.com). Many sites or programs offer parental controls.

Here are some popular kid-friendly web sites:

**www.askkids.com**

## www.kids.yahoo.com

## www.kol.com  (AOL's Kid's Online)

## www.zoobuh.com

When they get older you can negotiate an agreement with your kids outlining the rights and obligations of computer use at home.

Make sure the agreement clearly sets out:
- -where your kids can go online and what they can do there
- - how much time they can spend on the Internet
- -what to do if anything makes them uncomfortable
- -how to protect their personal information
- -how to be safe when communicating
- -how to behave ethically and responsibly while online.

Your children's input is critical to the success of the agreement. Print it out and keep it by the family computer to remind everyone of the rules. Review it regularly, and update it as your kids are older.

**How can I be sure the site is secure, if we want to shop online?**

If kids and teens shop online, they need solid guidelines to keep their transactions safe and secure. Only shop from trusted websites or companies. Some trusted online 'stores' are Amazon.com, Ebay.com, Paypal.com is a trusted payment intermediary. Teach them how to tell when it is all right to give credit information to a Web site by looking for: a Better Business Bureau quality assurance seal; an unbroken lock icon at the bottom left-hand corner of the page (ensuring that only you and the Web site can view financial transactions); or an "https" in the address box of your browser, which also ensures a secure environment.

Make sure your browser supports 128-bit <u>encryption</u> to ensure your credit card number is automatically encrypted, or scrambled, before it is sent. Some online users even have a separate credit card that they only use for internet transactions and monitor it frequently.

## How do I check for encryption?

When doing any personal business on the internet you want to have the information encrypted. Encryption means your information or data is translated into a secret code when it travels on the internet. Encryption is a very effective way to achieve data security.

Check your browsers address bar.

At the beginning of the websites address it could be   HTTP:// or HTTPS://

Unencrypted websites have the header   HTTP://

Usually – Protected and  Encrypted web sites start with  HTTPS://

Example:   **https://www.yourbank.com**

Depending on your browser – There should also be an little lock or Icon telling you if the site you are on is encrypted.

Internet Explorer 6 looks like this (bottom right of window):

Internet Explorer 7 has the lock near the top  like this:

By hovering over the little 'lock' it should tell you the strength of the encryption.

(128 bit is good, 256 or more is better)

When you click for more information, it sometimes tells you further about the encryption, the security certificate and which online Security Authority is used to secure the site.

This example:

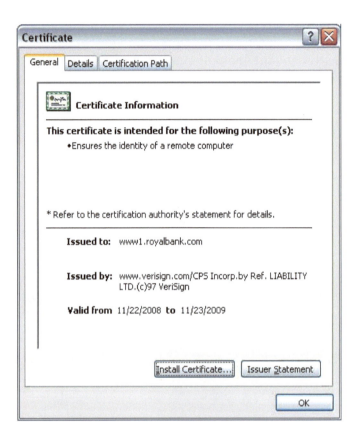

Verisign is a trusted source on the internet for security certificates.

## What should I look for in a Website's Privacy Policy?

When a website wants to collect information from their users, a Privacy policy outlines the privacy terms and conditions of a site.

If your child signs on to a companies website to access certain features, or purchase something or even to request information – it is important to know the web-sites privacy policy.

Be aware that some Web sites for children—even the most reputable ones—sometimes ask for e-mail and home addresses, telephone numbers, and parents' professions before allowing children to enter.  Often, however, these privacy policies are vague, misleading or non-existent.

When you read a privacy policy, you want to know:

- what information is being collected or tracked,
- how this information will be used
- whether it will be shared or sold to a third party
- do you have the ability to change or delete data collected from your children;
- what steps are taken to safeguard kids regarding activities on the site;
- does the site try to obtain verifiable, parental consent before a child releases personal information online?

Most links to privacy policies or privacy statements of web sites should be found on the home pages.

Yahoo's is here:

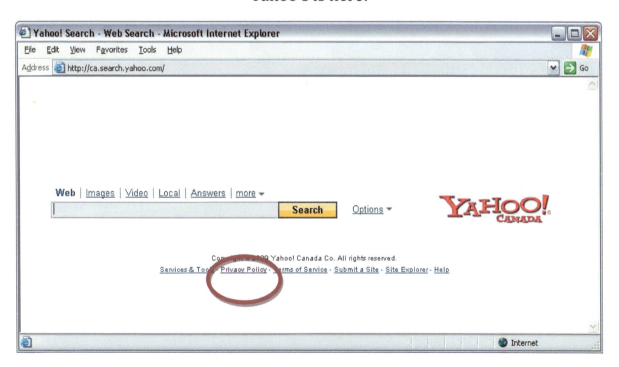

Microsoft's is here:

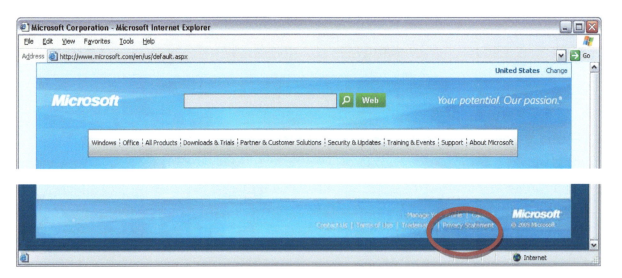

## What if.....?

Encourage your kids to come to you if they come across anything online that makes them feel uncomfortable or threatened.

When dealing with this situation remember:

    - Many times an inexperienced user doesn't mean to do anything wrong.

    - Often, people are tricked into clicking on something.

    -Sometimes, even a program or website can do things automatically.(like pop up a undesirable website or bring up a website that the user did not want.)

A very good suggestion is to stay calm. If you get upset - they may not turn to you for help when they need it. Just remember, it's very common for first time users to bring up a website or click something they didn't intend to.

## Searching……

A huge benefit of using the Internet is the amount of information.  Type in virtually any phrase of query into a search engine like Google or Yahoo! – brings you loads of information!
 But, care is needed when searching on the internet.  The biggest and most popular search engines are Google,  Ask Jeeves  or Yahoo!   Even these sites are not immune to the possible dangers.
Most offer filters to block adult  or inappropriate content.

Example of Google's SafeSearch Filtering:

(found in Google *preferences*)

Care and a little bit of education is needed when searching the internet.  Using Search engines to find valid and relevant information is somewhat of an art.  Today's search engines work very well in finding what you want but still, care is needed.

Words that have double meanings cause a lot of grief, embarrassment and problems for inexperienced (and even advanced) users.

Perhaps your child is researching a report and is looking for information:

"European  food".  Kids could type 'spicy sausage' and get adult content.

Watch out for other double-meanings as well.

ExpertsExchange.com could also mean  ExpertSexchange.com

Weed, Grass, Cookies,  or  Bill  ( which could refer to legislation, currency, ducks or that rich Microsoft dude.)

If  your young child has a project or a topic they want to search for, make sure you spend time with them and help them sift thru the many pages of information!

Example of a simple search for '**horses**' on Google:

Notice the results -  over  **101 million**  results or pages!!
You will have to refine your search.
Search again with more keywords – perhaps "raising and caring for horses"

# E-mail

f you have Internet access, you probably use e-mail.  Sending and receiving e-mail, which stands for electronic mail, is the number one use of the Internet. E-mail is a fast, efficient and cheap way for anyone  to stay in touch with people around  the world.

Despite the benefits, anyone who uses e-mail is aware of the explosion of spam, or junk e-mail, which floods into inboxes each day, much of it offensive or obscene. It has been estimated that junk e-mail makes up over 40 to 90 percent of all e-mail travelling over the internet.

Kids, who may not think critically about the messages they receive, are particularly vulnerable to the ads, scams and disturbing messages that can show up in their accounts.

Obtaining an email address is very easy  - many companies offer free email address's  and storage

Some of the most popular free email online services are Hotmail, MSN, Yahoo or Gmail.

**Privacy Note**: Keep in mind these email repositories or where the data is stored -  can be anywhere in the world (with different privacy laws than your country) – and can be very easily accessed by people other than yourself. )

Example of a web-based email address  **bob1980@gmail.com**

Where Bob1980 is your *username*  and *gmail.com*  is your host email domain or company.

Internet Service Providers (ISPs) also generally supply their customers with free e-mail accounts.

In Canada,  it could be   Telus,  Rogers, Shaw, Sasktel, etc.

If your kids are young, consider setting up a shared e-mail account for them so you can monitor their messages.

To protect young children from receiving unwanted messages, teach them to never share their e-mail address with anyone they don't know.

If your kids are older, they probably have their own free accounts through sites such as Hotmail and Yahoo!   Help them set up filters on these accounts to avoid unwanted messages and make sure that in the registration process they choose NOT to receive promotions from advertisers or to be included in an Internet directory.

Encourage them to protect their e-mail address and never give it out over the Internet. This helps  protect them from spam (unwanted advertising and perhaps nefarious email).

Often,  websites ask for an email address  before you can access certain information or get special offers.  Many people  don't feel comfortable giving out their real personal email address – so you can  Set up a 'dummy' e-mail account  to give out online.  You still can use this email address but its is only meant  for signing up for things and non-personal matters.   This will protect your real address from junk e-mail.

**Teach children be careful with e-mails from people they do not know**

Instruct your child never to open emails, (especially with attachments), from people they do not know. Most likely these emails contain a computer virus or they are mass mailing (spam) e-mails with inappropriate content.

**Giving  out personal information**

Instruct your kids never to give out personal information (name, address, telephone number, password, where you live, school name, credit card number, and so on)
Be aware that Web sites for children—even the most reputable ones—sometimes ask for e-mail and home addresses, telephone numbers, and parents' professions before allowing children to enter.

**Should  my children have their own e-mail accounts?**

Young children should share a family e-mail address rather than have their own accounts. As they get older and want more independence, you can give them their own address. The mail can still reside in your family inbox, so you can ask about any suspicious-looking messages they may get. Ask your Internet Service Provider (ISP) what options it provides for family e-mail accounts.

Most kids want to have their own e-mail accounts, and they'll have no trouble getting one through free services such as Hotmail or Yahoo! Make sure they take every precaution to protect their e-mail address so they don't receive junk e-mail and messages from strangers.

Even then, it would be wise or a parent to monitor their children's email accounts. This would mean you would have to know their username and password and then periodically checking their email activity. Also be aware its very easy for them to get a new secret email address – so communicate with your children.

**How to check email activity** – What to look for..

When you log on to an email account - there are folders where 'received', 'deleted' and 'sent' messages are stored or copied to.

Here is an screenshot of Microsoft's free email service (called Windows Live, MSN or Hotmail) and where certain folders and emails can be found.

(Other popular web-based email services have a different look but the same general folders that you can check)

After logging in with a username and password you should get to this screen:

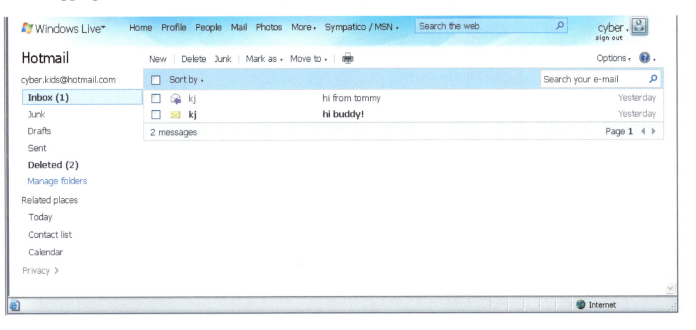

You can check what messages have been sent by clicking on the 'sent items' folder…

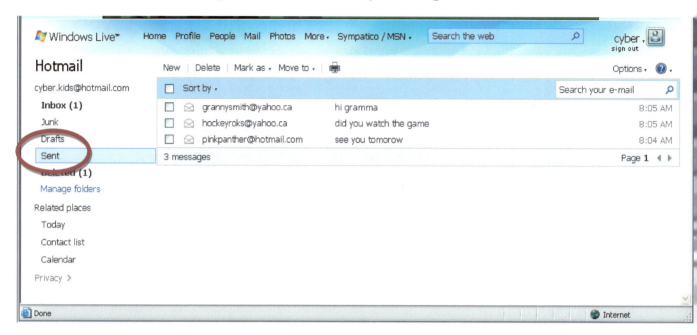

Finally you can check the deleted messages folder. (usually both send and received deleted messages go here before disappearing). Be aware it is possible for the user to delete messages from this folder as well.

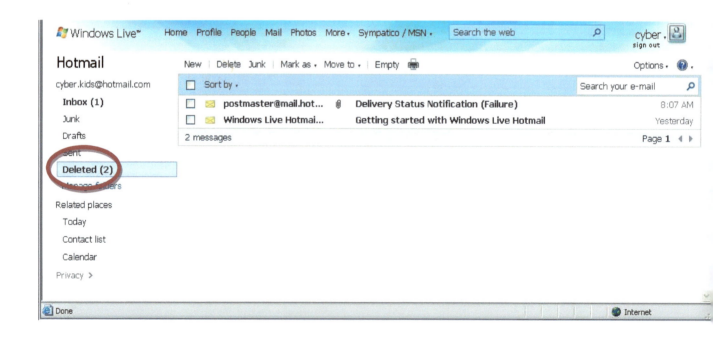

# Instant messaging

For today's computer-savvy generation, instant messaging (IM) has replaced the telephone as the most popular way of talking with friends. Kids rush home from school, log on and continue schoolyard conversations, often staying online for hours. Instant messaging is a great cost-free tool for kids to communicate with friends, and to keep in touch with people around the world.

Many parents confuse instant messaging with chat rooms when their kids say they are 'chatting' online. While both technologies involve communicating there are important differences that have safety implications.

There are many IM clients that can be used – most popular are MSN messenger, Yahoo messenger , AOL Instant messenger and Google Talk/Chat.

There are clients or software that allows typing messages but there are also ways to communicate using voice (with a microphone – just like a Internet Phone) or even Video feeds (using a webcam). Webcams are relatively cheap and are sometimes even built into newer laptops. This technology could allow anyone on the other end of the Instant Messaging conversation to see into your house!

A chat room is a place on the Internet where many people at once can talk to anyone in the world. Imagine opening up an international phone book, picking out random strangers and calling them. Instant messaging is a safer environment because it permits users to select the people they want to talk with. Users create contact lists of friends to chat with and can block people they don't know or don't want to communicate with.

While kids have some control over who they talk to, it's still possible to talk with strangers using IM. Some kids like having huge instant messaging contact lists – it means some kids have over 100 IM 'friends,' possibly many of whom they've never met.

Its very easy to obtain new contacts for Instant Messaging – some programs (called 'spiders' or 'robots') – are used to randomly discover usernames on IM networks and attempt to communicate with people, advertising products and services (some inappropriate).

Because of their familiarity with their computer - Kids can feel freer to say things online that they would never say face-to-face, so instant messaging can be used to spread rumors and gossip. For many kids, this means home also has the peer pressures of school. Cyber Bullying is becoming a growing problem.

**Privacy Concern** :  Most IM programs encourage users to fill out a 'personal profile' which includes detailed personal information. Once completed, this profile can be available to anyone on the Internet who wants to pull it up and read it.

Kids should be taught to never fill out these kinds of profiles online with their own personal information.

Also it is important to continue to review with your kids  - their contact list and outline what should never be released while Instant Messaging  (personal pictures or information.)

## Teach children about Netiquette

Good manners can protect kids, too.  Words written are just as strong as words spoken. Tell children never to respond to messages or bulletin board postings that are suggestive, obscene, or harassing. Ask them to be sensitive to others' feelings when posting online messages and to avoid being rude, mean, sarcastic, or excessively argumentative. A comment that's meant to be funny could seem insulting and make others upset. Visit websites  and chat rooms with your kids to point out comments that could be misinterpreted.

## Use nicknames instead of real names

A nickname—an online alias (like **HockeyKing** or **PinkLady22**)—is also vital to protecting privacy because it conceals a person's real identity.
It might help to make with your children a 'dummy' profile with imaginary information because some programs, websites or services require some information to sign up..
Consider sharing the same nickname and e-mail address with your younger children so that you can closely monitor the instant and e-mail messages that come to them.

# A better way to set up a profile:

Here is a screen shot of a Hotmail Email account (an account like this usually integrates with MSN messenger (popular IM client). Notice very little (if any) of the users personal information is entered:

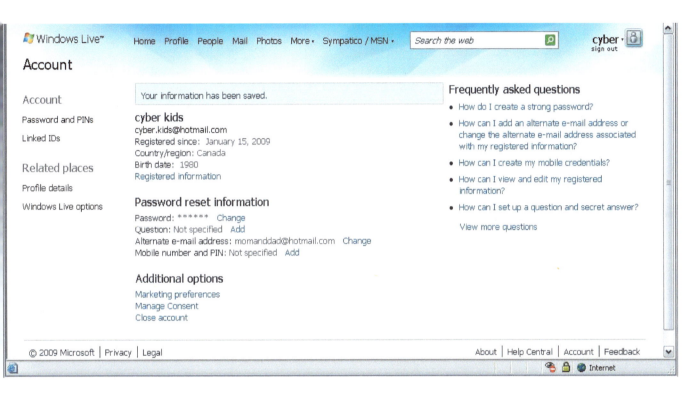

For example: the only information for the user is the name 'Cyber Kids', a country and a quite generic birth year.

## How old should my child be to use IM (Instant Messaging?

Many students instant message with friends on a daily basis, so denying access to this popular tool may place limitations on your child's social life. Once kids start using instant messaging, parents have an important role to play in ensuring their privacy is protected and they are using the technology responsibly.

Your IM rules should include:

- no filling out a profile with any of the child's personal information
- only chat with contacts that a parent and child know.
- never talk to strangers (you should check their contact lists regularly to make sure they know everyone on them)
- do not be involved with spreading rumors and gossip or hateful messages

## Can I read my child's Instant Messaging conversations?

Usually - Yes. Instant message chatting can be set up to automatically save 'chat logs' in a folder on your computer. Depending on the IM client, you can save IM conversations to a file that can be read with any word processing program.

If kids know about these logs, however, it's easy for them to go into "Options" and disable this feature.
In the end having good open dialogue with kids is much more constructive then spying on them. Kids may always be one step ahead of parents when it comes to technology. So - you need to get some good rules in place and trust that your kids will follow them.

There are ways for most IM clients to log the conversations or messages. Each different type of IM client or even version might store the logs in a different location:

For example in MSN Messenger 8.5 ( a popular IM program) the option to turn on logging is in: *Tools/options/messages*
with the 'automatically keep a history of my conversations' check box turned on.

And then usually the conversation logs can be found:
*\My Documents\My Received Files\USERNAME\History*

You can then read the logs and previous conversations (including the dates, times and the chat participants) using a word processor like Word, Wordpad or Notepad.

For other versions or IM programs – the **help** option should direct you how to turn on logging and where the conversations are kept.

# Are Webcams safe for kids to use?

In the last decade or so – computers have dramatically fallen in price.  In the late 80's a standard personal computer cost around $3000 - $4000.  Now entry level machines cost $400-500 and you get a monitor and usually a printer as well.   Extras (such as webcams) are also quite affordable.

Webcams are also becoming increasing popular with young people.

For safety and security reasons, Webcams **should not** be attached to computers in kids' rooms where their use can't be monitored.

It's important to establish house rules for Webcams including:
- only  use the Webcam with people you know and trust .
- always keep the lens cap closed or unplug the Webcam from the computer when not in use.  (some spyware can turn on the camera without the user knowing it)
- never do anything in front of a Webcam that you wouldn't want the entire world to see.
- don't post Webcam videos on the Web.

There are a few viruses out there that can actually turn on the web cam,  and have a 'remote control' like hold on your unprotected computer.

In the 1990's there was a famous  hacker group 'Cult of the Dead Cow' that published a program called Back Orifice.  When a machine was infected - this tool allowed hackers to perform all kinds of mischief -- including opening and closing CD-ROM drive doors and switching on webcams.

In 2004, a new virus called RBOT  took spying on victims one step farther than most worms -- this malicious program is capable of switching on webcams and send the information(images)  elsewhere, and allowing the author to literally peek into victims' lives.

What can you do to prevent this?  Keep your computer up to date with patching and anti-virus.  More on that later!

# Chat rooms

Chat rooms are places on the Internet where you can have live conversations with many people at the same time. Think of it as a telephone party line - except you type rather than talk. Everyone in the chat room can see what everyone else writes, but you can still be as anonymous as you want.

While chat rooms can be dynamic meeting places for people with similar interests, they can also be cruising grounds for predators trying to make contact with young people.

For this reason, kids should not be in public chat rooms - period. Just as we teach young children not to talk to strangers in the street, they shouldn't be talking with strangers online. When they become older they should only participate in monitored kids' chat rooms, and even then under the close supervision of an adult.

Chat rooms are monitored in several ways. Some sites run software that automatically shuts people out for using inappropriate language, while others use real live monitors

Keep in mind that even in monitored chat rooms, there is nothing to stop an adult from joining in and pretending to be a child.

Young teens are particularly vulnerable with regard to chat rooms. They're trying to gain some independence and want to move away from parental control.

They also may want to explore the world and to establish new relationships outside the family.

In the anonymous atmosphere of chat rooms, they feel free to be more open and honest and conversations can quickly become intimate, making them vulnerable to online predators.

Because of this, adolescents should be encouraged to only use monitored teen chat rooms, to protect their personal information when chatting online and to always stay in the chat room's public area.

 (Some chat rooms offer users the option of going into 'private' rooms, or sharing private messages, that no one else can see or monitor.)

Keep your Internet-connected computer in a public area of your house - never in a child's room.

**Never to have online profiles with real information**

Instruct your kids never to have online profiles with any personal information. This means they will not be listed in directories and are less likely to be approached in children's chat rooms, where pedophiles often search for prey.


**Never allow a child to arrange a face-to-face meeting with someone they met online.**


Instruct children to never arrange a face-to-face meeting with another computer user without full parental permission and involvement.
Never allow them to get together with someone they "meet" online without first checking this "friend" out to the best of your ability.
If a meeting is arranged, make the first one in a public place, and you must accompany your child.
Thus, someone indicating that "she" is a "12-year-old girl" could in reality be a 40-year-old adult.

This is a real threat:

Here is an excerpt from **www.cybertipline.com**.

Millions of children engage in chat and instant messaging every day and the overwhelming majority are not victimized. But - Of the 32,000 leads reported to the National Center for Missing and Exploited Children's (NCMEC) CyberTipLine: 3,262 are ``online enticement'' cases and the vast majority of those started out in a chat room, according to Ruben Rodriquez, director of NCMEC's Exploited Child Unit. However, the fact that they represent a tiny fraction of kids online is of no conciliation to those children or their families.

# Blogging

A blog (which comes from the term "Web log" or "weblog") is a Web application which contains posts like a diary or journal entry.

There are many blogging sites popular with kids that allow users to create profiles containing diary-type postings, photos and even videos.

Blogs are a snap to create and easy to update, making them extremely popular . National Syndicated News agencies are advertising and using blogs to disseminate information .

It is widely believed that the 2008 United States election winner President Obama used blogs and social networking sites to gain support.

It is common nowadays for many human resource departments in companies to search blogs and social networking sites. They do this to research prospective employees and their activities. Because of the way the internet is designed - It is very hard to remove unwanted pictures or videos. They could be cached (or saved) on many computers for years to come.

The popularity of blogs has also created a demand for "fake blogs" in which a company will create a fictional blog as a marketing tool to promote a product.

Several blog search engines are used to search blog contents, such as Bloglines, BlogScope, and Technorati.

Sites, such as Twitter, allow bloggers to share thoughts and feelings instantaneously with friends and family and is much faster than e-mailing or writing.

 Blogging sites that are popular with Canadian students include Nexopia, Piczo, Facebook and LiveJournal.

Problems can arise if kids post personal information, photos or video of themselves on these sites or if they use their blogs to spread rumours or gossip about peers and teachers.

Kids need to be reminded that anything posted on the Internet is accessible to anyone and could potentially be available online for years, so they should be careful that their blog doesn't include any personally identifiable information or images, rude or threatening comments or anything that could be embarrassing to themselves or others.

# File-sharing

File-sharing, also known as "peer-to-peer" technology, allows users to search for and download files from other users' computers. Using Torrents is another popular way of sharing files.

Young people use this technology to swap music files or video files of TV shows and movies. Kids have embraced downloading culture from the start, and, as with most technologies, are way ahead of parents in this area.

Even the average computer user could easily research and find how to download almost any movie, tv program or music video/song.

Some popular software that enables file sharing can be Limewire, Kazaa, UTorrent, Bitlord, or Bitcomet.

Parents need to take an active approach in this area and discuss the ethics of file-sharing with their children. It is a complex topic, with many people, including parents, downloading files and some musicians speaking out in support of the practice.

You can help your kids think about this issue by asking if they're aware that file-sharing is illegal. Ask them to think about the artists who created the work. Should they not be compensated when their songs are exchanged online? Also, if everyone file-shares where will the money come from to develop and promote new artists?

You could even wind up in a costly lawsuit and the computer's owner.

To access a file-sharing network, users need to download and install special software.

While these programs are available free online, they come at a cost. Some of the most popular programs are bundled with additional software known as "spyware," or "adware."

Once installed on your computer, this software can track where you go on the Internet, creates links on Web pages that send users to advertising and even collect information from your hard drive such as passwords, credit card numbers and email addresses.

Another concern related to file-sharing is that many people use these networks to trade pornographic images and videos, making it easy for kids to stumble across obscene material.

(Many times pornographic images or videos are 'disguised' as popular songs or videos)

Compounding the problem is the fact that parental filters designed to block pornography don't work with file-sharing programs.

Some file-sharing programs now offer their own built-in filtering systems, so check to see if the program your kids are using can be configured to block sexually explicit material. (More on this - in the 'What is my child doing on the Internet?' chapter.)

## What are the dangers of File Sharing?

As well as all the legal and moral implications.   You are opening your computer and possibly your personal data to the Web.   Perhaps you don't care that your vacation pictures are viewed by the file-sharing community. But you definitely don't want all your Word documents, financial software files and other personal data accessible to strangers.

Most  file-sharing programs work the same way. After installation, they establish a folder to store downloads.  The user can designate the specific folders for sharing. It's awfully easy to select a folder that contains private data.  Some peer-to-peer programs don't create a special folder for shared files. They use the My Documents folder and its subfolders. That's where most people store personal data and images.

Shared folders are inherently dangerous. It's easy to store files in the wrong folder. All the security software in the world won't protect you if you give strangers access to your files.

If you have peer-to-peer programs, remove them. Parents and grandparents should check their computers if children have access to them.

Kids can very easily install programs on a computer in less than 5 minutes. Then, after that, the programs can run in the background quietly.

Many have been blindsided by suits filed by the recording industry.

Most programs can be removed through Windows. Click Start, then Control Panel. Double-click Add or Remove Programs.  Highlight the program and click the Remove button.

Use Anti-virus programs and make sure they are up to date.  More information can be found in the 'Protecting  Your Home Computer' Chapter.

# Cell Phones

The mobile phone will soon be the most popular consumer device on the planet. About half of the 800 million phones sold in 2007 had significant processing power, broadband data connectivity, external storage, integrated cameras and multimedia playback.  This means that cell phones have a lot of features and a lot of potential.

This new generation of cell phones can  have Internet and text messaging capabilities and can take and submit digital photos and videos. These phones are challenging for a parent to monitor.   Unlike a computer placed in a public area of a home or school, cell phones are private,  always connected and easily accessible.

Text messaging, also known as SMS, for short message system is popular with kids because it's cheaper to send a text message than to make a phone call and they can send their message out to many people at the same time.

It's called short message system because cell phone screens are so small they can only display a limited amount of words. Kids use an SMS language, based on short forms and acronyms, that is also popular in chat rooms and with instant messaging. Cryptic conversations written in SMS lingo baffle most adults.

For example, here's a short conversation in SMS:

 **how wz d pRT last nyt?  Got 2 go, c U l8r**

Translation: **How was the party last night? Got to go, see you later.**

As with the Internet, parents and kids use cell phones differently. Most parents see cell phones as tools, while kids view them as an integral part of their social and entertainment lives.

Unlike parents, who find cell phones intrusive at times and turn them on and off as necessary, kids have their phones turned on all the time so they can always be reached - by their friends that is, not necessarily by their parents!

There are many easy to obtain and install applications for  newer cell phones – especially Apple's shiny IPhone.

Some applications can use a picture taken on a kids cell phone and immediately post it online to everyone on the internet to see!

Some phones can use Bluetooth technology with applications that scan and send beacons to complete strangers.. These beacons could include personal information and even come with an invite to talk!

An increasing number of kids are using their text messaging and camera-enabled cell phones to bully and harass peers. Because kids tend to keep their phones on at all times, bullies can relentlessly harass victims at school, at home or even in their own rooms. If your child is bullied through a cell phone, report the problem immediately to your phone service provider. If it's a persistent problem you can change the phone number.

## What should I do if my child is being harassed online?

If this occurs, you can 'block' the person sending the harassing messages. There are 'block' options in e-mail and instant messaging programs. Save any harassing e-mail messages and forward them to your child's e-mail service provider. Most providers have appropriate use policies that restrict users from harassing others over the Internet.

If the harassment consists of comments posted on a Web site, contact your Internet Service Provider (ISP) and ask for help to locate the ISP hosting the site. You can then contact the ISP and bring the offensive comments to their attention.

You should also contact your local police department. Harassment is a crime in many countries, both in the real world and on the Internet. It is illegal to communicate repeatedly with someone if your communication causes them to fear for their own safety or the safety of others.

# Social Networking Sites

Social networking sites are extremely popular with Canadian kids. Users create their own web pages and profiles on these sites, which often contain personal information and photos.

Most social network services are web based and provide a variety of ways for users to interact, such as e-mail and instant messaging services.

The use of social networking web sites such as MySpace, Facebook, Bebo, Classmates or Friendster  is very popular with many age groups.

But there are some problems:

In October 2006, a fake Myspace profile created in the name of Josh Evans by Lori Janine Drew led to the suicide of Megan Meier.  Megan was a 13 year old girl that committed suicide based on a boy that "dissed" her on a MySpace site.  The "boy"  (Josh Evans) was actually the mom,  Ms. Drew,  of an estranged friend.  Drew was convicted of three counts of accessing protected computers without authorization to obtain information to inflict emotional distress on Meier.

This  event incited concern regarding the use of social networking services for cyber-bullying.

The misuse of social networking services has led many to cast doubt over whether any information on these services can in fact be regarded as true.

**Should your kids be using blogging or social networking sites?**

While the age restriction is 14 years and older for Nexopia and 13 for Piczo and Do You Look Good, the content on these sites can still  be inappropriate for young teens.

If your kids are using blogging or social networking sites you should view their profiles and blogs to ensure that no personal information or photos have been posted.

If  you must have some family or personal information  on a website – it is possible to limit the access of people on the internet that can see your site.  Set up access lists and then only people that you have invited can see your social network profile.

Example:  Starting a Facebook profile requires you to sign up:

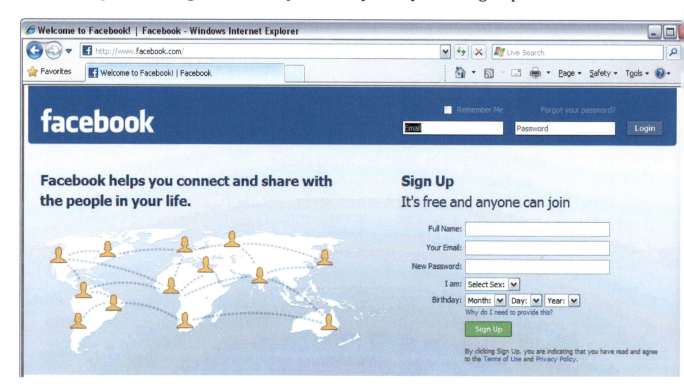

After logging on – there are more profile options that can be filled in. Its important to monitor what information your kids are entering…

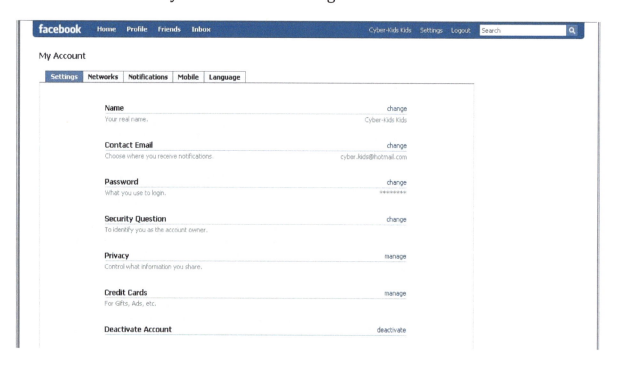

There are also some privacy options that you should look into that control:

-who can see your profile and information
- who can search for you and how you can be contacted
-how your profile interacts with other applications on Facebook.
-you can even block other users (within Facebook) from contacting you

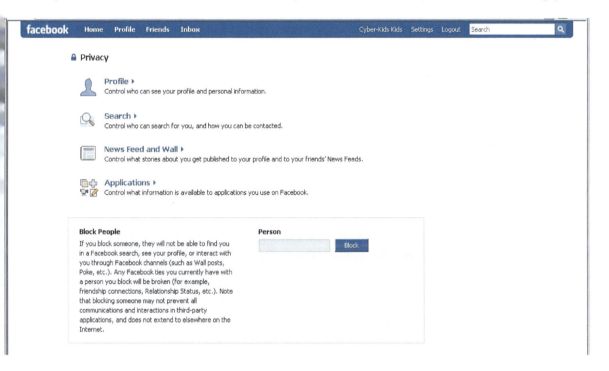

Make sure if you allow your children to have a Social Networking Page:

- You have access

- You can monitor what information is entered and who is allowed to view your kids web site

- It's not public (meaning anyone can view)

- Access to the site is invitation only and only for people you know and trust.

- Nothing personal or confidential is entered on the social website

# What is my Child doing on the Internet?

**Can I track my kids' Internet use?**

Yes, you can track where they've been online, but be aware that some computer-savvy kids know how to cover their Internet tracks. Clear rules about Internet use and open communication with your kids are more effective than invading their privacy or 'spying'.

When you surf the Internet, your Web browser collects information about the places you visit, and stores it on your computer.

Browsers usually keep 'history' files of recently visited sites. Most versions of Internet Explorer have a History button on the top toolbar. Double click on any listing to view the site. (see the example for Internet Explorer below)

Browsers also make temporary copies of Web pages, known as cache files, and stores them on your computer.

**How can I quickly check what websites have been visited?**

Each browser has a history or cache of previously visited websites.

For example:

Internet Explorer 6 has a history button:

This opens up a listing of what sites have been visited and when.

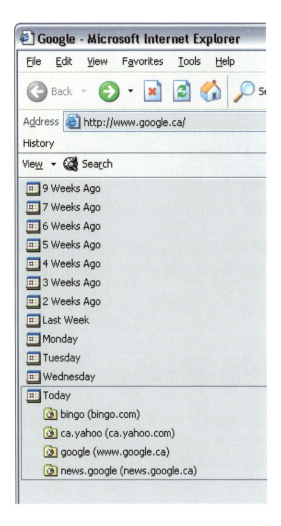

Double click on any listing to view that site.  Be aware – its fairly easy to delete this record of visited web sites.

## Internet Blocking and Filtering

There are programs available to you called Internet Filtering programs, which will run in the background on your computer while your kids are surfing the Internet.

These programs filter pornographic and other offensive content, monitor each surfer's online viewing , block access to certain web sites and newsgroups, keep kids out of risky chat rooms and log their online activities.

Combining the use of Internet Filtering programs with as much supervision as possible is the best method of protecting your child online.

Beware - There is a slight learning curve for the parent to keep the families computer up to date.

You will have to spend some time working on the computer in order to protect it properly

It might take a couple evenings of learning, reading and configuring the software. If this is too daunting there are many IT professionals that can assist you.

Then after its installed - a parent must monitor the situation weekly.

It is work – but it is important for a parent to be involved with their kids online activities!

Parents can choose from a variety of filtering and blocking software to help them control Internet content, access and activities. Some of the most commonly offered functions are:

**Blocking inappropriate content**

Software filters look for a number of things when blocking content: key words, originating server, a site's URL, even the amount of skin in the images on the page.

It is best to have a tool that uses a variety of techniques to block content rather than just key words - technologies cannot discriminate between unsuitable sites and innocent ones For example, many popular filters block Dykes Medical Library because the word "dyke" is slang for lesbian.

Filtering software is often ineffective with file-sharing or downloading programs. File-sharing networks are used to trade pornography because users can download directly from individual computers rather than having to go through a central server. Check to see if the filter you use works with file-sharing programs - some now do. Also, some file-sharing programs offer built-in filtering that you can set to block sexually explicit material

**Blocking or controlling program access**

Parents can choose to block access to all areas, or allow access only to certain monitored environments. ( chat rooms, e-mail or instant messaging).

## Monitoring computer use or Internet access

Many tools allow parents to track what kids do online, such as what sites are visited, and which activities, and for how long.  As your kids get older it is preferable to have open communication about their Internet use and clear rules about appropriate online behavior rather than using technology to invade their privacy.

## Preventing the transmission of personal information

You can program some software to recognize personal data, so if your child tries to type in personal information, the computer will not allow it  and dummy information would be entered.

## ISP parental controls

Many ISPs - companies that provide access to the Internet and its services (e-mail, downloading, chat rooms, World Wide Web) - now offer parental controls. Check with your ISP to find out if it offers filtered Internet access. Ask what criteria it uses to block sites.

## Computer shops

Most computer stores carry blocking and filtering software. Ask staff to explain the differences between various types of software, and to give you some installation tips.

## Does filtering software really work?

Filtering tools may be helpful with young children, to complement - not replace - parental supervision. Filters and blockers, however, are not foolproof and they can often fail to keep out inappropriate material.  They can also block a lot of useful content, which your kids may need for their school assignments.

While filters may be useful when your kids are young, as they grow older they will need to develop safe and responsible online behavior.

Once again -  Combining the use of Internet Filtering programs with as much supervision as possible is the best method of protecting your child online. Parents and teachers are best equipped to teach kids how to responsibly use the Internet.

# Protecting Your Home Computer

Just as you carefully watch what your family does, where they go, who they interact with, where they shop:   Protect, watch, and supervise your children online. Do not assume that your children are safe because they are in your home using a computer.

Use  firewalls, anti-virus, and spyware detection software on a regular basis. Be sure to download and install from the software manufacturer's website all available security patches and updates for all installed programs on your computer on a regular basis. If you don't feel comfortable or don't have time to install and update your machine – get someone competent to do so.   (If you don't know how to fix the lock on your front door – you wouldn't leave it unlocked for weeks or months?)

Make sure the computer is in a visible place in the house. Without acting confrontational, get involved &  ask questions. Walk by and check what is on the screen. If your child quickly closes the screen, this is  something that should be investigated.

## Spend time on the Internet with your children

Go online with your children as often as possible and help them identify inappropriate communications.
 Give them a chance to show you what they have learned or the things they like.
 Send E-Greetings and e-cards to family and friends or participate in interactive games together.
Ask your children to tell about their cyberspace friends, just as you would want to know their real-life friends.   Insist that your kids tell you first if they want to meet an "online friend."

Talk and educate  your kids about online pornography  and what it means. Discuss gambling and its potential risks and remind your teens that it is illegal for them to gamble online.

Teach your kids responsible online behavior. File-sharing and taking text, images or artwork from the Web may infringe on copyright laws. Talk about the problem of plagiarism.  There are websites that actually offer book reports that students can buy & download.

Be aware of the Web sites that your teens frequent, and make sure the sites don't contain personal photos and information or offensive content.

In general – spending time with your kids online can give you a good picture of what they know and what you can do and look out for.

## What should I know about computer viruses and spyware?

A virus is a malicious software program that infects computer files or disk drives and then makes copies of itself. Many of the activities that kids do online can leave computers vulnerable to viruses. E-mail attachments are the most common means of distributing viruses, but they can also be downloaded using file-sharing and instant messaging programs.

Make sure your children understand:

- to never open an e-mail when don't trust or know who it's from..
- to never open an attachment that they haven't asked for (sometimes a friend or family members computer can get infected and then 'spoof' or fake a message to you. This is how advanced viruses get around.)
- to configure their instant messaging program so they cannot receive files from other users
- to never download files ending in 'exe' or 'bat' when using file-sharing programs
- to never download any software or program off the Internet without checking with a parent first (many programs are portrayed as fun or helpful games – but have a sinister intent you don't see. This is malware or spyware. )

## What about Anti-virus software?

Every computer that in on the internet must have protection. You can protect your computer by always running up-to-date and anti-virus software. Some popular Antivirus companies are McAfee, Norton, Symantec, Kapersky, ESET and Computer Associates.

## How to check your virus is up to date / signature

Depending on the Antivirus program used – there is a date associated with the programs definition, signature or database of threats. Essentially that means your computer is protected from threats that originated before that date.

## How do I check the signature date?

Each Antivirus program – has their own location to find the threat protection date. Here are a couple examples of what to look for.  Kapersky Antivirus and F-Secure.

You will notice in both of the Anti-virus programs shown: They have the definition settings in a date form.

Kapersky looks like this:

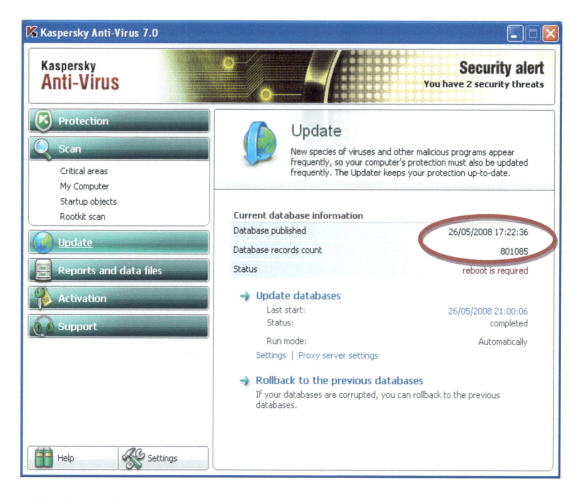

This example shows the computer  is protected for known threats up to May 26, 2008 (26/05/2008)

F-Secure looks like this:

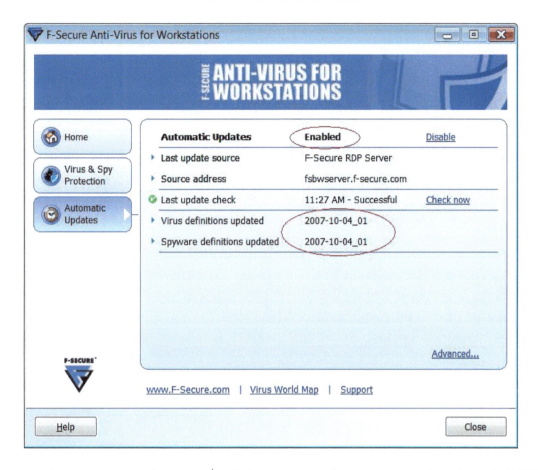

This shows us the computer is protected for known threats up to October 4, 2007 (04/10/2007)

Your signatures or definitions should be no older than a week from your current date.

Make sure **auto-update** of the signatures is enabled and working.

## How can I prevent pop-ups on my computer?

Pop up's are small windows or websites that load usually without the users intention. Sometimes they serve a purpose (more information or a side point when researching) But other times they are advertisements or even worse – invitations to nefarious websites.

When a person is surfing the internet, it is very common to see misleading advertisements that invite a user to click on them.

Some examples of 'Bad Pop-ups' that could take a user to problematic web sites. (advertising, malware, spyware, even adult-content)

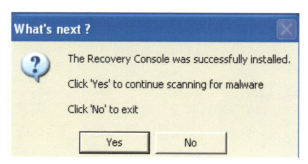

The easiest way to avoid pop-ups is to use pop-up blocking software that you can download or buy. Microsoft Windows Xp service pack 2 has a built in pop-up blocker but most people prefer to use more protection than that.


## Are Toolbars safe?

Some people like to use a specialty "toolbar" with your browser. Some toolbars have a search feature or a favorite website link feature. Many toolbars allow you to click on a button to block pop-ups, and then click again to disable the pop-up blocking feature. There are privacy issues around using specialty toolbars, however, because they can be used to trace your Internet tracks. Some worse toolbars (or so they claim) install programs that change your computer settings to add favorites, change your home page and even bring up websites with advertising (or worse). Usually these toolbars have ads that are customized to your browsing habits – sometimes they even send your personal information to the internet. Generally if you are concerned with your privacy (which you should) - avoid toolbars.


## What is Anti-spyware/Malware

Anti-spyware/Malware programs should be installed, updated and run on a regular basis.

Spyware and Malware are programs that run in the background = often without a users knowledge. They can have varying degrees of harmfulness. These types of programs could simply keep a bit of information about a users browsing habits or they could be a key logger that keeps track and sends exactly what a user types and does on their computer.  Personal information, credit card info and other personal information is a valued commodity for computer hackers and identity thieves.

Updating and scanning using Anti-spyware programs regularly, can cleanse your machine of any such unwanted software.

Microsoft provides one called Windows Defender, it's a free install for Windows XP machines and should come with Vista automatically.

After updating the signatures (meaning to have a list of the most current threats) the anti-spyware scanner  will identify programs that are  suspicious and clean or neutralize them or even give you the option to delete, quarantine, or leave them alone. (sometimes there is a program  that may be mis-identified and you want it left running.)


**Am I Infected by spyware or malware?**

Usually,  a user that is familiar with their home computer knows when something has changed or it is acting 'funny'.  Sometimes it is very hard to tell.

Here are some symptoms to look for:

- When you start your computer or at any random time, your Internet browser opens to display Web site advertisements.
- When you use your browser to view Web sites, other windows open to display advertisements.
- Your Web browser's home page  changes.
- Web pages are unexpectedly added to your Favorites folder.
- New toolbars are unexpectedly added to your Web browser.
- You cannot start certain programs.
- When you click a link in a program, the link does not work.
- Your Web browser suddenly closes or stops responding.
- It takes a much longer time to start  your computer.
- Components of Windows or other programs no longer work.

If you suspect any of the above – get your computer cleaned by a competent computer technician.

## What is a Firewall?

A firewall is a security program that has rules to prevent unauthorized electronic access to your computer. It could take the form of am installed program on your computer. It could also be part of your Internet router or modem (that connects your computer to the internet). Every computer or network that is on the internet should have a running and up to date firewall. Most people use the one that Microsoft provides for Windows XP and Vista machines.

## What is Phishing?

Another growing problem on the internet is 'Phishing'. This is a form of fraud that is carried out over the Internet when using e-mail. Phishing attempts are designed to trick the user into disclosing personal and financial information and typically appear to come from well known and trustworthy websites or from a specific email address "spoofed" to appear as though it has come from a legitimate person.

Skilled hackers can craft an email and a website to appear to be legitimate.

Some common web sites that are frequently spoofed by fraudsters are Ebay, Paypal and many banks. A user could receive a convincing email that their account needs some attention and they should go to the website listed and enter their username and password.

The website that the link went to looked like a legitimate web page, but in reality, was a phishing site where personal and account information was gathered.

There are many examples of Phishing attempts. They can be from Banks, Stores, Online Services, Paypal, E-bay, Microsoft, Lottery corporations, Medical Sales, Online Prize Giveaways……..

Be wary of any emails that want you to enter any personal information.   Check every web site link that you are invited to click on.   A big reason that Phishing works so well is a website can appear to look legitimate.  Looking closer however,  the actual address of the spoofed website is incorrect.

**Example**:

An  email that appears to be from your bank asks you to verify and enter personal information.  It even provides a  link  for you to click on :

How you can check where the link goes:

By hovering (not clicking) your mouse pointer over the link…….

You can see the actual destination on the bottom left part of the browser window.

Yikes!  The link actually doesn't go to www.bankofamerica.com

It says www.bankofamericaportal.com – a slightly different address  but a completely different website.

Teach your kids to be  very careful and stay away (don't click) from scams like these.

# Reporting Internet Abuse

**Reporting Dangerous Online Situations or Child Pornography**

If a child is in immediate physical danger, call 911 or your local police.
If a child or teen is being stalked, harassed or threatened online, contact your local police.

If a young person is in danger of being lured into a real-life meeting with possibly a predator call your local police.

There are also many help websites or help lines available:

US Department of Justice: www.usdoj.gov

Canada : www.rcmp-grc.gc.ca

www.cybertip.ca or use the toll-free phone line: 1-866-658-9022

Wired Safety : www.wiredsafety.org

You should also report any such incidents to your Internet Service Provider (ISP).

If the incident involves a fellow student, contact the school principal as well.

**Fraud**

In Canada you can report directly to the RCMP.

by using its Reporting Economic Crime Online (RECOL) site at

www.recol.ca or use their toll-free phone line: 1-888-495-8501.

The United States Government has a good starter home page: www.usa.gov

You can report Internet fraud www.usa.gov/Citizen/Topics/Internet_Fraud.shtml

Remember to keep any evidence related to your complaint.

# Conclusion

The Internet is an interesting place for kids. It can be a lot of fun and an exciting way to communicate with friends and family. It also can be a wealth of information. Even learning how to use it properly and safely - can be a valuable skill in today's high-tech world.

By applying real-world parenting skills and remedies to the cyber-world, you can make the Internet a safe place for your family.

As with many avenues of parenting – the more time that you spend with your children, the more rewarding the whole experience of the Internet can be, and the more their safety is ensured.

Remember, Internet use is a privilege that can be taken away if misused.

Hopefully, this book has educated you on the very interesting and diverse Cyber-space!

You also should be able to use this knowledge to help protect your family when it comes to using computers and the internet.

Have fun out there – but also stay safe!

# References & Helpful Websites:

Here is a source listing of more information and websites about Internet Security and Protection of families.

Kid-friendly sites, Managing the Internet at Home , Technological Tools
www.bewebaware.ca

A parent's guide to safe, simple, kid-friendly e-mail
http://www.pcworld.ca/news/column/59486a20c0a8000601afdbbb8bfa4d2b/pg0.htm

Public Safety Canada's website
http://www.publicsafety.gc.ca

SafeCanada.ca - Internet Safety
http://www.safecanada.ca

Google's Tips for Online Safety
http://www.google.com/intl/en/landing/familysafety/

Young Canadians in a Wired World
http://www.media-awareness.ca/english/research/YCWW/phaseII/index.cfm

Office of the Privacy Commissioner of Canada
http://www.privcom.gc.ca

USA  Federal Trade Commission

http://www.ftc.gov/bcp/menus/consumer/tech/privacy.shtm

On Guard Online

http://www.onguardonline.gov/

www.ingramcontent.com/pod-product-compliance
Lightning Source LLC
Chambersburg PA
CBHW041423050326
40689CB00002B/630